Centre for Baptist History and

Occasional Papers V

Text and Story
Prophets for Their Time and Ours

Gale Richards

Foreword by Stephen C. Jennings

Regent's Park College, Oxford

Regent's Park College is a Permanent Private Hall of the University of Oxford

Copyright © Gale Richards 2014

First published 2014

Centre for Baptist History and Heritage,
Regent's Park College,
Pusey Street,
Oxford.
OX1 2LB
(Regent's Park College is a Permanent Private Hall of
the University of Oxford.)
www.rpc.ox.ac.uk

The right of Gale Richards to be
identified as the Author of this Work has been asserted by her
in accordance with the Copyright, Designs
and Patents Act 1988

All rights reserved. No part of this publication may be reproduced, stored in a retrieval system, or transmitted in any form by any means, electronic, mechanical, photocopying, recording or otherwise, without the prior permission of the publisher or a license permitting restricted copying. In the UK such licenses are issued by the Copyright Licensing Agency, 90 Tottenham Court Road, London W1P 9HE.

British Library Cataloguing in Publication Data
A catalogue record for this book is available from the British Library

ISBN 978-1-706632-29-0

Front cover illustrations:
Images of Martin Luther King, Jr, Mojola Agbebi,
Helen Burroughs, Sam Sharpe, and Peter Stanford.
. Used with permission.

Typeset by Larry J. Kreitzer

Contents

Foreword by Stephen C. Jennings 1

Preface   Text, Story and the Sam Sharpe Project 3

Introduction and Explanation 5

Study 1. Martin Luther King, Jr. The Prayer Life of
    a Prophet 7

Study 2. Mojola Agbebi. Identity Matters............. 14

Study 3. Nannie Helen Burroughs. Taking the
    Initiative........ 21

Study 4. Sam Sharpe and Strategic Resistance... 28

Study 5. Peter Thomas Stanford. Reaching Out to
    the Margins 35

Foreword

Interesting. Informative. Interactive. Intellectually stimulating. Theologically sound. Bible grounded. Culturally conscious. These are some of the several adjectives that come to mind when one reads this book, Text *and Story,* written by Gale Richards. Compelling narratives, telling the true life-stories of five Christians of African Heritage who lived in Britain, the United States of America, Nigeria and Jamaica during the nineteenth and twentieth centuries, are complemented by ample illustrations and study questions. This makes the book an easy read for the conscientious reader or hearer.

And yet though it is written simply, this book is not simplistic, but profound. It is actually a resource engaging in conscientization. The term conscientization was made popular by Brazilian, Paulo Friere, and refers to the educating of ordinary people about life through everyday methods such as storytelling, song, dance and drama with a view to empower them to transform their lives, circumstances and contexts in liberating ways. In this resource, Gale Richards is engaging in conscientization, in raising consciousness about the history of African and African Diasporan persons of the Black Atlantic, with the hope that that history will be a source of inspiration to those who engage with it.

Of particular interest is the way in which the Biblical passages cited by the writer for us readers to use, are the very ones already used by the protagonists/heroes/icons/saints/persons featured in the work. Gale's special skill is to allow us to be involved in a fusion of horizons, to find and link the viewpoint of the original world of the biblical text and its context, with that of the contextual and textual world of the hero of a previous generation, along with that of the implied world of our current context and a possible interpretation and application of the text and its context to ours. All of this happens without our necessarily knowing this, through her deceptively simple prose and through its engagingly interactive style.

This work deserves the widest readership and usage, not just in Britain but throughout the world. I am sure that persons of Black African Heritage in Europe, Africa, North, Central, and South America, and the Caribbean will find the work particularly useful as some of the issues faced by the African and African Diasporan Christians mentioned in the book still exist. It should therefore resonate well with this kind of reader, not just at the level of the problem, but at the level of the God-inspired resolution made possible through a proper, Spirit-led utilization of the Christian Scriptures.

Please read: enjoy and be edified.

Stephen C.A. Jennings
September 2014

The Revd Dr Stephen C. A. Jennings is an ordained and accredited minister of the Jamaica Baptist Union (J.B.U.). Pastor of the Mona-Circuit of Baptist Churches in Kingston, Jamaica, he is also a part-lecturer (adjunct professor) of Caribbean and Contemporary Theologies at the United Theological College of the West Indies. The Dr Jennings is a former President of the J.B.U., and was the President in 2008, when the Baptist Union of Great Britain and the Baptist Missionary Society came to Jamaica to offer a formal apology to the Jamaica Baptist Union for the British role in the Atlantic Slave Trade.

Preface
Text, Story and the Sam Sharpe Project

The study materials that follow, under the heading 'Text and Story', form one part of 'The Sam Sharpe Project – for education, research and community building'. The project is named in honour of The Right Excellent Sam Sharpe, a National Hero of Jamaica, who was an enslaved person, Baptist deacon, and the organizing genius behind the 'sit-down strike' of Christmas 1831 which made a major contribution to the ultimate abolition of slavery in 1833. The project was launched at the Jamaican High Commission on 10 May 2012, at the kind invitation of the High Commissioner, and as part of the celebrations of 50 years of Jamaican independence.

The project not only supports historical research into the life of Sam Sharpe, but is also intended to provide educational opportunities in local churches. In particular, it aims to encourage adults and young people to discover their potential for leadership in church and society today. Several programmes are running within the orbit of the Project, including an annual lecture which last year (2013) was given by the Revd Neville Callam, General Secretary of the Baptist World Alliance, speaking on the themes of the continuing need to 'deconstruct the notion of race', and on the continuing threat of racism within churches and society.

The 'Text and Story' programme within the project takes its inspiration from the fact that Sam Sharpe was motivated in his actions by reading Scripture, being impressed by such texts as the saying of Jesus that 'no one can serve two masters'. It becomes clear, on only a little enquiry, that other Baptists who struggled against marginalization and oppression to become leaders in their community and to make a significant impact on their society were similarly influenced by Scripture.

The programme encourages adults and young people to reflect on the story of these pioneers, on the scriptural texts that shaped them, and on their own stories today in order to find their place in society and develop their potential for leadership.

The Steering Committee of the Sam Sharpe Project was delighted to commission one of its members, Gale Richards, to develop the vision for this programme, and to bring the idea into reality by writing a series of study notes. Few could have been so well qualified to undertake this task. Gale, whose parents are Jamaican, is a Project Development Worker with the Heart of England Baptist Association, and is already working with congregations to develop the skills and gifts of adults and young people in different parts of Birmingham, England and its environs. At the same time she is a tutor for Northern Baptist College, helping students and church leaders to reflect theologically on their context. With an academic training in criminal justice, youth and community work and Applied Theology, she brings a wealth of insight to studies which bring together life stories and the biblical passages associated with them.

I commend these studies and hope they will be widely used to help a new generation to discover the gifts God has given them, and to use them in our church and society today.

Paul S. Fiddes
Principal Emeritus, Regent's Park College, Oxford.
On behalf of the partners of the Sam Sam Sharpe Project:

Jamaica Baptist Union
Oxford Centre for Christianity and Culture
BMS World Mission
Faith & Society Team, Baptist Union of Great Britain
Heart of England Baptist Association
London Baptist Association
Northern Baptist College
Bristol Baptist College
Dr Delroy Reid-Salmon (Founding Partner)

Introduction and Explanation

As I have reflected on my own spiritual formation, I have realized that hearing about and reflecting on the life stories of key Christian figures has played a major role in my formation. It is their lived-out experience that has helped me bridge the gap between the example of Christ I read about in the Gospel accounts, and my understanding of what being Christ-like in thought, word and action might look like, in today's church and society.

I am not alone in believing that the stories of lived-out Christian faith are hugely important in the spiritual formation of individuals and communities. There is the key work of two American theologians – James W. McClendon Jr, who explores the concept of *Biography as Theology*,[1] and Anne Wimberly who develops the power of 'story linking' in her book *Soul Stories*.[2] In addition there is the work of the Black British theologian Anthony Reddie, who explores the power of story, especially in drama, in his *Dramatizing Theologies*.[3]

This *Text and Story* resource seeks to build on the work of such writers on life-stories. It proposes that it is important not only to reflect on the lives of key Christian figures, but also on the understanding of particular key biblical texts that these individuals used to underpin their thinking and actions, as suggested by historical accounts of their careers.

My hope is that many others will explore the potential for the spiritual formation of individuals and communities through reflection on both the lived-out experiences of key Christian figures (in the form of biographies), and on the biblical texts they drew insights from.

---

[1] James W. Mclendon Jr, *Biography as Theology. How Life Stories can Remake Today's Theology* (Oregon: Wipf and Stock, Oregon, 2002).

[2] Anne Wimberly, *Soul Stories: African American Christian Education* (Nashville: Abingdon, 1994).

[3] Anthony Reddie, *Dramatizing Theologies: A Participative Approach to Black God Talk* (London: Acumen, 2006).

The study material in this resource particular focuses on the life stories of pioneering Baptist leaders such as Sam Sharpe, who experienced social marginalization and even oppression while living in contexts as diverse as the Caribbean, West Africa, North America and Britain. Yet, despite these circumstances, they helped to bring about groundbreaking change in their societies.

I must extend my grateful thanks to Israel Olofinjana for writing the Mojola Agbebi biography[4] and Paul Walker for writing the Peter Stanford biography, which enabled me to develop the Bible study material pertaining to both of those featured key Baptist leaders.

This resource thus encourages participants in study groups to reflect on these life stories and associated biblical texts, to consider what relevance they have to their own sense of history, identity and potential for leadership.

As I piloted some of these studies with young people in the summer of 2013 and with adults in summer of 2014, all of whom were from a range of ethnic and cultural backgrounds, many have said they have found the studies inspiring. My prayer is very much that those who make use of this resource will find awakened within them their gifts for leadership, in order to bring about a transformation within society today.

---

[4] Copies of the biographies featured in this resource are downloadable from: www.samsharpeproject.org

Study 1. Martin Luther King, Jr.
The Prayer Life of a Prophet

Martin Luther King, Jr. Artist: Jack Lewis Hiller, 1960
National Portrait Gallery. Used by kind permission.

Opening Prayer

The person leading this prayer might like to base it around a biblical text that has a particular focus on justice, such as: Psalm 146 or Micah 6:8.

Introduction

Give a response to the following questions:
- What age were you when you first heard about Martin Luther King Jr (MLK Jr)?
- What do you know about MLK Jr?

Make a note of your answers.

The story of Martin Luther King

- Watch a short film telling the life story of MLK Jr, for example the ones produced online by cloudbiography.com or biography.com.
- Then read the short, written biography of MLK Jr on the pages that follow this study.
- Once you have done this, reflect on whether there is anything new that you have found out about MLK Jr from the clip or the biography.

Martin Luther King's connection with the prophetic books of the Bible

In MLK Jr's *Letter from Birmingham Jail*[5] to clergy (Jewish and Christian leaders) who were not supporting the Civil Rights Movement, MLK Jr actually likens himself to eighth-century BCE prophets such as Amos when accused by these clergymen of being an 'outsider coming in' to the Birmingham area. MLK Jr asserts that:

> 'I am in Birmingham because injustice is here. Just as eighth-century prophets left their little villages and carried their "thus saith the Lord" far beyond the boundaries of their hometowns ... I too am compelled to carry the gospel of freedom beyond my particular hometown'.

MLK Jr again seems to be modelling himself on eight-century prophets like Amos, when in his 'I have a dream' speech he puts Amos 5:24 into a new framework for his own day, as follows:

> 'No, no, we are not satisfied, and we will not be satisfied until "justice rolls down like waters, and righteousness like a mighty stream".'

---

[5] To read a copy of the *Letter from Birmingham Jail,* see: www.americanrhetoric.com.

The actual wording of Amos 5: 24 is: 'But let justice roll on like a river, righteousness like a never-failing stream!'[6]

Lewis V. Baldwin in his book *Never to Leave us Alone – The Prayer Life of Martin Luther King Jr.*[7] also establishes that MLK Jr felt a strong connection to the book of the prophet Jeremiah, and in particular, Jeremiah 12: 1-6 and Jeremiah 17: 14 and 18. Take the time to read those particular texts in Jeremiah and keep the following questions in mind:

- Who is the text being addressed to?
- What behaviour is being deemed unacceptable?
- What behaviour is being deemed acceptable?
- Why might MLK Jr. have been drawn to those particular texts?

Some things we know about Jeremiah

The book covers the period from the early 7th century to the 6th century BCE (perhaps something like 627 to 580 BCE). We can determine this from the different kings who are mentioned as ruling whilst he is prophesying throughout the book.

Jeremiah delivers messages to the Southern Kingdom of God's people some years before its destruction. Jeremiah warns them that they are forsaking God and predicts that Babylon will not only defeat the people of Judah but will take its inhabitants off into exile primarily in Babylon. However, he offers assurance that after some 70 years a number of the people of Judah will return and rebuild.

We know that Jeremiah is prophesying over a number of years to God's people but gets very little positive response from them: in fact he is publicly mocked and beaten (Jeremiah 20:7), receives death threats (Jeremiah 11:19), is imprisoned (Jeremiah 32:1-5) and is instructed by God not to marry or have children (Jeremiah 16:2).

---

[6] Holy Bible. New International Version
[7] L. V. Baldwin, *Never to Leave us Alone – The Prayer Life of Martin Luther King Jr* (Minneapolis: Fortress Press, 2010), pp. 32-33.

Why Martin Luther King found these texts in Jeremiah to be so important

We see from MLK Jr's *Letter from Birmingham Jail* that he understood his role as being akin to that of the Old Testament prophets. He identified himself as a prophet and so would obviously have identified with the sufferings of prophets like Jeremiah. He too was taking his message to those who were supposed to be God's fellow disciples (remember, his letter from Birmingham jail was written to Christian clergy).

Thus, he like Jeremiah would have wanted to know how to cope with the suffering he was enduring and so could see that one way of doing that was, like Jeremiah in chapters 12 and 17, to take even his 'rawest' of feelings to God in prayer. His assumption was that prophets, or any disciples, were doing this not to condone any ungodly feelings within them but rather to release such feelings and to hand them over to God. His hope must have been that the outcome would be, as in the case of Jeremiah, that God would respond to his prophets' prayers by reviving them, by enabling them to continue to speak and act prophetically, which in the case of MLK Jr was to further the Civil Rights Movement.

The relevance of Martin Luther King's story for 21st - century life

How helpful do you find MLK Jr's intention to be like Jeremiah, and to bring even the 'rawest' of his feelings to God in intimate prayer?

Do you think for example, that you too might find such an approach to prayer helps you cope with ridicule or other forms of attack you might be on the receiving end of, for practising your Christian faith? Might it actually enable and sustain you in having a prophetic voice and taking prophetic action on some of the injustice we see happening in today's society?

Spend some time reading through some current news items and consider what an appropriate prophetic voice or action might look like for at least one of those issues. Then consider what role you might potentially play in helping to bring about a more just response.

In thinking about what an appropriate response to the issue might look like, do remember that what was key to the success of the Civil Rights Movement, led by individuals like MLK Jr, was that those actually being oppressed played a pivotal role in the struggle for their own freedom. This is a process sometimes referred to as 'conscientization'[8] and 'liberation from below.'

Closing act of worship

Listen to or sing the song 'There is a balm in Gilead.'[9] It is a song believed to be inspired by a combination of the biblical texts Jeremiah 8:22 and 1 Peter 2:24, and it was sung during the Civil Rights movement. It is a song that can remind us today too, that no matter how difficult serving God may seem at times, God will revive us and provide us with the wisdom we need to move forward and bring about change. In doing so we build on the legacy that individuals like MLK Jr have left us.

******

Biography of Revd Dr Martin Luther King, Jr

Martin Luther King, Jr, (January 15, 1929-April 4, 1968) was born Michael Luther King, Jr in Atlanta but later had his name changed to Martin. Both his grandfather and father were pastors of the Ebenezer Baptist Church in Atlanta where Dr King also went on to serve as co-pastor.

King Jr attended racially segregated public schools in Georgia, graduating from high school at the age of fifteen; he received the BA degree in 1948 from Morehouse College, a black college in Atlanta.

---

[8] This term was developed in Paulo Freire, *Pedagogy of the Oppressed* (New York: Continuum, 1970).
[9] There is a Nina Simone version of this song on *You Tube* or on her 'Baltimore' album, or see www.hymnary.org for lyrics and music.

He went on to study at Crozer Theological Seminary in Pennsylvania where white and black students mixed freely on campus, even sharing dormitories. This mixing was not on occasion without the incidence of some racial tensions but King Jr is reported to have made some close relationships with white students. In 1951 he enrolled in graduate studies at Boston University, completing his residence for the doctorate in 1953 and receiving the degree in 1955. In Boston he met and married Coretta Scott. They went on to have two sons and two daughters.

In 1954, King Jr became pastor of the Dexter Avenue Baptist Church in Montgomery. King was, by this time, a member of the executive committee of the 'National Association for the Advancement of Colored People' (NAACP), the leading organization of its kind in the nation.

In 1955, Dr King accepted the leadership of the first great nonviolent demonstration by a boycott of buses in the fight for civil rights for black people in the USA. The boycott lasted 382 days. On December 21, 1956, the Supreme Court of the United States had declared unconstitutional the laws requiring segregation on buses, with black and white people sitting separately.

In 1957 he was elected president of the Southern Christian Leadership Conference, an organization formed to provide new leadership for the Civil Rights Movement. It is said that the ideals for this organization were taken from Christianity, while its non-violent resistance operational techniques were taken from Gandhi.

In the eleven-year period between 1957 and 1968, Dr King travelled all over the world speaking out against injustice and promoting non-violent resistance. He also wrote five books as well as numerous articles. In these years, he led a massive protest in Birmingham, Alabama, which received worldwide coverage, and inspired his *Letter from a Birmingham Jail*. He planned the drives in Alabama for the registration of black voters. He directed the peaceful march on Washington, D.C., of 250,000 people to whom he delivered his address, whose keynote was 'I Have a Dream.' He spoke with

President John F. Kennedy and campaigned for President Lyndon B. Johnson. He was arrested more than twenty times and assaulted at least four times.

Dr King was awarded five honorary degrees, was named Man of the Year by Time Magazine in 1963, and became not only a leader of American black people but also a world figure. He campaigned with and for people of a range of faith and ethnic backgrounds around justice issues. In the midst of achieving all of this, King was not without his personal struggles with reports that he sometimes turned to alcohol for comfort and found challenges in resisting extra-marital affairs.

At the age of thirty-five, Martin Luther King, Jr was the youngest man to have received the Nobel Peace Prize. When notified of his selection, he announced that he would turn over the prize money of $54,123 to the furtherance of the Civil Rights Movement. On the evening of April 4, 1968, while standing on the balcony of his motel room in Memphis, Tennessee, he was assassinated.

Further Reading

Nobel Lectures, *Peace 1951-1970*, Editor Frederick W. Haberman (Amsterdam: Elsevier PublishingCompany, 1972). Accessible on http://www.nobelprize.org/nobel_prizes/peace/laureates/1964/king-bio.html.

Richard S. Reddie, *Martin Luther King Jr: History-Maker* (Oxford: Lion Hudson, 2011).

Study 2. Mojola Agbebi. Identity Matters

Mojola Agbebi. Used with thanks from the Special Collections,
Royal Colonial Institute Photographic Portraits.

Opening Prayer

The person leading this prayer might like to base it around a biblical text that has a focus on 'diversity' such as: Revelation 7:9.

Introduction

Give a response to the following question:
- In what year do you think the first Baptist church in Nigeria led by Africans themselves was formed?

Make a note of your answer.

The story of Mojola Agbebi

- Read the short, written biography of Mojola Agbebi, which appears on the next few pages of this resource.
- Alternatively, if you are doing this Bible study with others you might want someone to do a dramatized reading of the biography of Mojola Agbebi, perhaps with African drums playing quietly in the background.
- After you have read and or heard the biography of Mojola Agbebi, reflect on whether or not you were surprised about the actual year the first African-led Baptist church in Nigeria was established.

Mojola Agbebi's connection with Acts 8:26-40

The story of Philip and the Ethiopian eunuch is very much associated with the establishment of the first churches with native Africans leading them in West Africa. Indeed many of these churches were described as being part of 'Ethiopianism.'[10] Ethiopianism was a term used to describe people of African descent seeking to reclaim their religious and political freedom from European colonial rule over many parts of Africa. They appealed to Psalm 68:31, 'Ethiopia shall soon stretch forth its hands unto God', but the mention of Ethiopia in Acts 8 was also influential.

Take the time to read Acts 8:26-40 and keep the following questions in mind:

- Why might it be significant that the person Philip was talking to was from Ethiopia?
- Why might the position the Ethiopian held be significant?
- Why might it be significant that having shared the gospel with the Ethiopian, Philip leaves him?

---

[10] For further detail on this see: Koschorke and others (eds.), *A History of Christianity in Asia, Africa, and Latin America, 1450-1990. A documentary source book* (Michigan: Grand Rapids, 2007), pp. 216-219.

- Why do you think early African Baptist leaders like Mojola Agbebi would have placed such significance on this story in their quest to establish and grow African-led churches?

Some things we know about the Book of Acts

The book follows on from where the Gospel of Luke ends and starts by telling us about Jesus' ascension to heaven and the coming of the Holy Spirit. It then depicts what the life of the early church was like. In Acts 6 we read about the choosing of seven leaders ('deacons'), including Philip, to initially serve at tables and distribute food, as a way of assisting the apostles. It is when we get to Acts 8 that we see that Philip, as one of those seven leaders, is now operating as an evangelist, as we see him meeting with the Ethiopian eunuch.

Why Mojola Agbebi might have found Acts 8:26-40 to be so significant

The term 'Ethiopian' in Scripture most likely referred to an area south of Egypt called Nubia, which we would now class as in southern Egypt and northern Sudan. In the Old Testament this region was called Kush, which essentially means that the eunuch would have been African (typically coming from that region, black in skin-colour).

The Ethiopian had gone to Jerusalem to worship. In those times there were two types of people who were interested in Judaism and wanted to be part of Jewish worship but had not been born or married into Judaism. First there were 'proselytes', or people who were converted to Judaism and had been circumcised. Second, there were 'God-fearers', or people who attended the Jewish synagogue and read the Jewish scriptures but did not get circumcised.[11] It seems most likely that the Ethiopian, as a eunuch, would have been regarded as a 'God-fearer.'

---

[11] For further background information on the text, see: J. L. Gonzales, *Acts: The Gospel of the Spirit* (New York: Orbis, 2001).

He is referred to in the text as an important officer of the Queen of the Ethiopians. This would have meant that the Ethiopian had influence. His voice would have been heard if he spoke of coming to Christ when he returned to Ethiopia.

Philip by baptizing this Ethiopian is potentially opening up the gospel to an entirely new nation. Further, since Philip left the Ethiopian after baptizing him, he did not go on to train him as a disciple, and this points to the Ethiopian having to find ways of expressing the gospel in Afrocentric ways for himself. That would leave individuals like Mojola Agbebi to conclude that 'native' or indigenous churches must have been God's desire, and consequently that the gospel can and should be expressed in different cultural styles, as God values cultural diversity.

Such a reading of the text would have gone against the thinking of many North American and European missionaries who went to places like Africa in the nineteenth century, and who often rejected all elements of the native culture without taking the time to consider whether much of it actually was 'anti' or 'contrary' to Christianity.

The relevance of the story of Mojola Agbebi for 21st-century life

Identify a current issue that relates to the failure to value cultural diversity.

For example, recent research in the UK has showed that job applicants with more British-sounding names are more likely to get job interviews than those with names that don't sound British. In a BBC news article,[12] Jorden Berkeley, a black 22-year-old university graduate from London, tells her story of spending four months applying for jobs but getting no responses from bigger companies, and offers from elsewhere that were limited to unpaid work experience. Then a careers adviser suggested Miss Berkeley drop her first name and start using her middle name, Elizabeth. 'I did not really understand this, seeing as my name isn't stereotypically "ethnic" or hard to pronounce, but it was worth a try and I changed it anyway,' she

---

[12] See: 'Whitened job applications' at http://www.bbc.co.uk/news/uk-20608039.

said, 'and I have been getting call-backs ever since.' She added: 'I have many, many friends who were effectively told to "whiten" their CVs by dropping ethnic names or activities that could be associated with blackness.'

Consider what an appropriate prophetic voice and action might look like on the issues you have chosen, bearing in mind the example of the life of Mojola Agbebi. Do also consider what role you might personally play in bringing that prophetic voice and action to the issue. Remember again that what was key to the success of the ministry of people like Mojola Agbebi was that those being oppressed played a key role in the struggle for their own freedom, sometimes known as 'liberation from below'.[13]

Closing act of worship

Listen to or sing a West African, Yoruba Christian worship song such as 'Igwe[14],' before closing with a prayer that gives thanks for twentieth-century leaders like Dr Mojola Agbebi, and the legacy they have left us to build upon.

******

Biography of the Revd Dr Mojola Agbebi
(by the Revd Israel Olofinjana)

Mojola Agbebi was born in Ilesha (now known as Osun State, Nigeria) on the 10th of April 1860, and originally was given the European name of David Vincent Brown.

At eight years old, he was sent to a Church Missionary Society (CMS) school in Lagos. He attended this school until 1874, after which he attended the CMS training school for three years. At the age of

---

[13] See footnote 7 above.
[14] See www.africangospellyrics.wordpress.com for lyrics and a link to a group singing the 'Igwe' song

seventeen in 1877, he became a CMS school-master at Faji Day school and continued in this role until 1880.

He later became involved with the First Baptist Church in Lagos founded by American Baptists. Here he became one of the first native African leaders alongside the ordained African pastor, Revd Moses Ladejo Stone. Moses Stone was later dismissed by the American Baptist missionaries, for taking on a trade to support his life as a pastor. Together with other native Africans like Mojola Agbebi, the pastor felt mistreated by the American Baptist missionaries, so they moved on from their church and founded the first African Baptist Church in Nigeria in 1888, which was known at the time as 'The Native Baptist Church', the term 'native' here meaning indigenous or national.

The Revd Moses Stone became the leader of this church and Mojola Agbebi served alongside him. He introduced the people of the Native Baptist Church to the idea of being self-supporting and self-governing. Mojola Agbebi encouraged the congregation to retain their African names, wear native dress and generally embrace African culture.

Mojola Agbebi began to wear exclusively African as opposed to European clothing and while in Liberia in 1894 changed his name from David Vincent Brown to Mojola Agbebi, as a mark of his appreciation of African culture. Additionally he made attempts to connect Christianity with African institutions and customs. He did this by instructing converts in local languages and in the appreciation of African arts and music. He strongly believed that if European missionaries had taken time to understand African culture it would have helped with the spread of Christianity among Africans.

He was a keen writer and was invovled in editing newspapers in Nigeria. In 1889, he published a small book entitled, 'Africa and the Gospel'. In this pamphlet, he argued for the creation of African churches. He declared, 'To render Christianity indigenous to Africa, it must be watered by native hands, pruned with native hatchet and tended with native earth ... It is a curse if we intend for ever to hold at the apron strings of foreign teachers, doing the baby for forever.'

In 1903 and 1904 he toured Britain and USA lecturing on African customs. He would wear his Agbada (Yoruba clothing) even in the cold weathers of Britain and the USA. Among the places he lectured and visited was the University of New York, where he received an honourary Doctor of Divinity Degree.

In 1908, he married Adeotan Sikuade and they had several children, to whom they gave African names.

In 1910, he co-founded with others the Lagos auxiliary of the 'Anti-Slavery and Aborigines Protection Society'. This was a group that spoke up about the needs of Nigerians before the British colonial government. He became the Vice-President of this group. Politically active, he presented a paper at the 1911 First Universal Races Congress in London

In 1914 the Native Baptist Church and its church plants reunited with the American-founded Baptist churches, to form the Yoruba Baptist Association, which was later to become the Baptist Convention of Nigeria. Mojola Agbebi was chosen as its first president.

Mojola Agbebi died on 17th May 1917.

Further Reading:
Mojola Agbebi, 'Inaugural Sermon', Lagos 1902. Text accessible on: http://www.blackpast.org/1902-rev-mojola-agbebi-inaugural-sermon.
E. A. Ayandele, *The Missionary Impact on Modern Nigeria 1842-1914: A Political and Social Analysis* (London: Longman, 1966).
Adotey Bing, Jonathan Derrick, and Godwin Matatu (eds.), *Makers of Modern Africa: Profiles in History* (London: Africa Books, 1991).
J. A. Omoyajowo, *Makers of the Church in Nigeria 1842-1947* (Lagos: Nigeria, CSS Bookshop, 1995).

Study 3. Nannie Helen Burroughs. Taking the Initiative

Nannie Helen Burroughs. Library of Congress: LC-USZ62-79903

Opening Prayer

The person leading might wish to base this prayer around a biblical text that emphasizes the importance of helping others, such as: Hebrews 13: 1-3.

Introduction

Give a response to the following question:
- The first worldwide gathering of Baptists took place in 1905 in London, England. Since then, gatherings known as the 'Baptist World Alliance Congress' have taken place every five years or so. In what year do you think the Congress had its first black female keynote speaker?

Make a note of your answer.

The story of Nannie Helen Burroughs

- Watch a short film telling the life story of Nannie Helen Burroughs, for example the one entitled 'A Deanwood Legacy' which can be found on *You Tube*.
- Additionally read the short, written biography of Nannie Helen Burroughs contained in the next few pages of this resource.
- After you have read the biography of Nannie Helen Burroughs reflect on how surprised you were (or not) about the actual year the Baptist World Alliance Congress had its first black female keynote speaker.

Nannie Helen Burroughs' connection with the Gospel of John

In her writing titled '12 Things the Negro Must Do for Himself and 12 Things White People Must Stop Doing', she argues that it is God's plan 'that the strong shall help the weak, but even God does not do for people what people can do for themselves.'[15] She was of course using the language of that time when she referred to 'the Negro,' a term that today is rightly regarded as derogatory.

Nannie Helen Burroughs goes on to illustrate 'what people can do for themselves' by urging that black people '…will have to do exactly what Jesus told the man (in John 5:8) to do – "Take up your bed and walk."'

Take the time to read John 5: 1-47 and keep the following questions in mind:

- Who is the text being addressed to?
- What behaviour is being deemed unacceptable?
- What behaviour is being deemed acceptable?
- Why might Nannie Helen Burroughs have been drawn to this particular text?

---

[15] Note: she actually wrote: 'what man can do for himself.'

Some things we know about the Gospel of John

The other three Gospel accounts by Matthew, Mark and Luke are referred to as the Synoptic Gospels. This is because they include many of the same stories, as they seek to cover the major events of Jesus' ministry.

The Gospel account of John misses out many of the events that are covered by the Synoptic Gospels. However, John focuses on what the Synoptic Gospels do not (at least, not in detail) – namely Jesus' trips to Judaea to observe the Jewish festivals such as the Passover. Three different Passover feasts are recorded in John (John 2:13, 23; John 6:4; and John 11:55) whereas the Synoptic Gospels focus on the one Passover celebrated during Jesus' final days on earth. Thus the religious life and spiritual condition of this community in Jersualem is a key focal point of the account in John's Gospel.

The Gospel of John is also well known for the 'I am' statements by Jesus found within it, which emphasize the divinity of Jesus. The 'I am' statements are linked to seven strong metaphors or pictures: 'I am the bread of life (6:35)', 'I am the light of the world (8:12)', 'I am the gate for the sheep (10:7)', 'I am the good shepherd (10:11)', 'I am the resurrection and the life (11:25)', 'I am the way, and the truth, and the life (14:6)', 'I am the true vine (15:1)'.

Why Nannie Helen Burroughs may have found this text in the Gospel of John to be so important

The 'I am' statements provide a very 'strong' image of Christ. Nannie Helen Burroughs as a Christian and therefore a follower of Christ's example seems to see the need for Christians to also be very 'strong' in their actions.

We know that a Jewish festival is taking place at the beginning of John 5 but we are not told which one. It is in the context of this festival that Jesus heals a man who has been sick for 38 years. The healing takes place on the Sabbath, which the Jewish leaders oppose.

We also know that Jesus denies that the man has been sick and disabled for 38 years because of his own sinfulness (See John 9:2-3). Rather, Jesus is urging the man to experience not just physical healing but also spiritual health in moving forward.

The key point that Nannie Helen Burroughs appears to take from the text is the role the man plays in his own physical and spiritual healing, in that he needs to be 'strong' and 'rise, take up his bed and walk.' For her, the key point appears to be that God works through people, and even those in need have to be 'strong' and help themselves up and out of the situation they find themselves in.

The relevance of the story of Nannie Helen Burroughs for 21st-century life

Identify a current issue that relates to the failure to care for those on the margins of society. For example, consider the lack of practical and financial support available for young people from poor backgrounds who are experiencing high unemployment levels during periods where there is an economic downturn, and therefore a genuine shortage of available jobs.

Then consider what an appropriate prophetic voice and action might look like on the issues, and what role you might personally play in bringing that prophetic voice and action to bear on the issue. Remember to bear in mind the example of the life of Nannie Helen Burroughs.

In doing this, also reflect on the limitations of Nannie Helen Burroughs' assertion that those who are marginalized need to seek to help themselves. In particular, consider the fact that some people may simply not be in a 'strong' enough position to be able to help themselves up and out of the situation they find themselves in. What clues might other aspects of her story give to finding a way forward here?

Closing act of Worship

Listen to or sing the song 'Can't give up now' by the American Gospel group Mary Mary. It is a song that reminds us that today, we must not give up on struggling for a more just society, just as black people like Nannie Helen Burroughs did not.

Close with prayers, asking for God to provide us with the courage and wisdom to build on the legacy left us by individuals who have lived through the past two centuries, such as Nannie Helen Burroughs.

******

Biography of Nannie Helen Burroughs

Nannie Helen Burroughs was born on 2nd May 1879, in Orange, Virginia, USA. Her mother, Jennie, was born an enslaved person, and had been freed after the ending of the American Civil War, becoming a cook. Her father, John, was born free, and combined being a farmer and a Baptist preacher. She moved to Washington DC in the early 1880s.

As a teenager she helped to found the 'National Association of Coloured Women', to give women the strength of banding together to advance in life. She also began to edit a Christian newspaper (*The Christian Banner*). In 1900 she shot to national fame for a stirring speech at the Convention of the National Baptists, called 'How the Sisters Are Hindered from Helping'. The Women's Convention auxiliary to the National Baptist Convention was formed not long after she gave that speech. In 1905, she went on to be a keynote speaker at the first Baptist World Alliance Congress, which was held in London, England.

In her twenties she saw the need for education among young black women to remove the hindrances they faced, and in 1909 founded the 'National Training School for Women and Girls' in Washington, D.C.

The school aimed to give students qualifications to prepare them for employment. Burroughs offered courses in domestic science and secretarial skills, but she also broke barriers by offering training for occupations in which women were not usually to be found at that time – examples were shoe repairing, gardening and men's hairdressing. She believed that where women were doing domestic work, this should be professionalized and regarded as a vocation. She aimed for all her students to become self-sufficient wage-earners and was an active leader in the 'National Association of Wage Earners', working to influence legislation related to wages for domestic workers and other positions held by women. She followed her own advice by taking a course in business studies, and later received an honorary master's degree.

For ten years she worked as a finance officer and editorial secretary for the Foreign Mission Board of the National Baptist Convention alongside her work in the school. She emphasized to all her students the importance of being proud black women, teaching African-American history and culture through a required course.

She urged black men and women to create businesses, which would appeal not only to other black people but white people as well. She thought they should aim to advance their community by adopting the highest standards in business and everyday life. Her message about working hard and not relying on mere handouts from others was important for the time, when black people were just beginning to create wealth after years of being enslaved. It was essential for African-Americans to make a place for themselves in American society.

During the time of the 'Great Depression' in the USA, when many people became homeless, President Hoover appointed her as a committee chairwoman in his White House programme for home building and home ownership.

In 1934 her school was renamed the 'National Trades and Professional School for Women', reflecting the status it gave to women. The Great

Depression closed it down for a while, but she fought to re-open it and succeeded.

In later life Burroughs offered support to Martin Luther King, Jr in his struggles for civil rights for black people in the USA. During the Montgomery bus boycott in 1956 she wrote to King's mother, Alberta, expressing her interest in the 'calm, sure way that Junior is standing up for right and righteousness.'

Nannie Helen Burroughs died in 1961. In 1975 the mayor in Washington D.C. declared 10 May to be ''Nannie Helen Burroughs Day'.

Further Reading
Nannie Helen Burroughs Project – an educational campaign: www.nburroughsinfo.org.

Article, 'Nannie Helen Burroughs' in *The Martin Luther King, Jr Research and Education Institute* Papers, Accessible at: http://mlk-kpp01.stanford.edu/index.php/encyclopedia/encyclopedia/enc_burroughs_nannie_helen_1879_1961/.

Evelyn Brooks Higginbotham, *Righteous Discontent. The Women's Movement in the Black Baptist Church, 1880-1920* (Harvard: Harvard University Press, 1993).

Study 4. Sam Sharpe and Strategic Resistance

Sam Sharpe. Jamaica Information Services.
Used with thanks

Opening Prayer

The person leading this prayer might base it on a biblical text that has a focus on justice, such as: Psalm 146 or Micah 6:8.

Introduction

Give responses to the following:
- Name as many Christian figures as you can think of who were involved in fighting for the abolition of the transatlantic slave trade.
- What do you know about the Jamaican Baptist deacon Sam Sharpe?

Make a note of your answers.

The story of Sam Sharpe

- Read the short, written biography of Sam Sharpe contained in the next few pages of this resource.
- Alternatively, if you are doing this Bible study with others you might want someone to do a dramatized reading of the biography of Sam Sharpe, perhaps with African drums playing quietly in the background.
- After you have read and or heard the biography of Sam Sharpe, reflect on what new things you have found out about Sam Sharpe.

Sam Sharpe's connection with the Gospel of Matthew

Historical accounts suggest that Sam Sharpe was greatly influenced by the text in Matthew 6: 24, where Jesus is recorded as telling hearers that 'no one can serve two masters', going on to say that 'you cannot serve God and wealth'.

Take the time to read aloud Matthew 6:19-34. You may also wish to listen to this text as recorded in the Jamaican New Testament version of the Bible.[16] As you read and or listen to the text, have the following questions in mind:

- Who is it that Jesus is addressing his words to?
- What behaviour is Jesus deeming unacceptable?
- What behaviour is Jesus deeming acceptable?
- Why might Sam Sharpe have connected this text to the need for the abolition of slavery in Jamaica?

Some things we know about the Gospel of Matthew

This is the Gospel account that has the most references to Old Testament texts, and seeks to enable us to see how the Old Testament

---

[16] See www.soundcloud.com/biblesociety/sets/jamaican-audio-new-testament for an audio version of the New Testament in Jamaican.

story links to the life and teaching of Jesus. This also enables readers to see that the God of the Old Testament is the God portrayed in the New Testament.

In the early chapters we see Jesus performing his miracles and by the time we get to chapter 11, we see Jesus delivering stinging criticism against the cities where he did most of his miracles, because the people choose not to change their lives and stop sinning. Whilst Jesus' ministry was about bringing wholeness and health to people and society, the Jewish people he was talking to were buying into the motivations of Roman rulers who controlled their land. Their own behaviour was being influenced by Roman practices of ruthlessly acquiring status, wealth and power (empire building) often through unjust taxes, rents and other unfair trading practices.

The religious rulers of the people of Israel such as the Pharisees were coming up with all sorts of interesting interpretations of the laws God had given the people of Israel to live by (for example, resting on the Sabbath meant no healing on the Sabbath!), which all helped ensure the poor remained poor, and the sick remained so in society.

Why Sam Sharpe might have found this text in Matthew to be so significant

It seems that Sam Sharpe believed that the ultimate 'master' of a human being should be Jesus. This must have entailed a criticism of the institution of slavery where slave-owners claimed an absolute mastery over the enslaved persons they 'owned'.

Further, he saw that the slave-masters in his context were caught up in trying to serve the God of the Bible while at the same time serving another god, which he recognized as the god of wealth. It was this god of wealth that enabled them to justify the oppressive enslavement of human beings.

Sam Sharpe may also have picked up on the fact that the book of Matthew is full of examples, which enable us to draw similarities between Moses' experiences and those of Jesus. For example:

- Pharaoh killed all the baby boys of the people of Israel, and only Moses is saved (Exodus 1:22 – 2:10); so also Herod (the King of Israel at the time of Jesus' birth) kills all the baby boys in Bethlehem, and only Jesus is saved (Matthew 2:13-18).
- In Matthew 4:7 when Jesus is being tempted he quotes Deuteronomy 6:16 and thus echoes Moses when he says to the people of Israel 'You should not test the Lord.'
- At the end of his life Moses commissions Joshua to go into the Promised land and to observe all the commandments in the law, and Joshua is assured God will be with him. At the end of Jesus' time on earth, Jesus commissions his disciples to go and make disciples all over the world and to observe all he has taught them, and he promises to be with them always.

The connection of Matthew's Gospel with the Old Testament, and particularly its echoing of themes in the life of Moses, reminds us that Moses served a God who freed his people from oppression and slavery. Moses himself led the exodus of Israelite people out of slavery in Egypt. This character of the Gospel may well have aided Sam Sharpe in seeing the significance of this saying of Jesus in Matthew 6:24 for bringing about liberation from the slavery he experienced in his time.

The relevance of Sam Sharpe's story for 21st-century life

In Sam Sharpe's time it was black people that were not being treated fully as human beings, but rather regarded as objects to be used and abused. In today's society, we can reflect on others who also suffer this way, and among them the millions of girls and women in the world who are not being treated fully as human beings, but who are used and abused as they are subjected to gender-based violence.

In 1993 the United Nations, in its *Declaration on the Elimination of Violence against Women,* [17] developed a definition of gender-based violence which sets out the fact that this can take the form of: domestic violence (in the home); cultural violence (perpetrated by the

---

[17] See:http://www.endvawnow.org for full details of the definitions.

wider community) and state violence (perpetrated by government officials).

Consider what an appropriate prophetic voice and action might look like on the issue of gender-based violence today, bearing in mind the example of the life of Sam Sharpe. Do also consider what role you might personally play in bringing that prophetic voice and action to bear on the issue.

In thinking about what an appropriate prophetic response to the issue might look like, consider: what 'master' is it that those committing gender-based violence are serving? For example, is it the god of wealth, power or sex?

Do also remember that what was key to the success of the ministry of people like Sam Sharpe was that those being oppressed played a pivotal role in the struggle for their own freedom. In the story of Sam Sharpe communal Bible study and prayer played a key part in this process, sometimes referred to as 'liberation from below.'[18]

Closing act of worship

Listen to the Jamaican National anthem,[19] which is a prayer. Then conclude by giving thanks for 19th-century prophets like Sam Sharpe and the legacy they have left us to build upon.

******

Biography of The Right Excellent Sam Sharpe

Sam Sharpe was born in the St James area of Jamaica. The precise year of his birth is unknown (limited records were kept of those born into slavery). Available records suggest he was born around the year 1800.

---

[18] See footnote 7 above.
[19] See: www.nationalanthems.info for lyrics and music

He was given the name of his enslaver Samuel Sharpe and he was used as a domestic slave (as opposed to a slave working in the fields), to attend to the domestic needs of his enslavers.

Sam Sharpe went on to attend the Baptist church in the Montego Bay area of St James. Thomas Burchell, a white British Baptist minister, pastored this church. Sam Sharpe in time was given the role of a leader (deacon) in the church. His leadership role at times included leading the church when his pastor Thomas Burchell was abroad.

Sam Sharpe is recorded as becoming known as 'Daddy Sharpe' and 'Ruler Sharpe' within the community of enslaved people, both traditional titles of respect and leadership. He was also later called 'Preacher to the rebels' by those outside.

In 1831, Sam Sharpe is recorded as planning and organizing a non-violent protest against slavery in the form of a 'sit-down' strike, which would involve those who were enslaved refusing to work after the Christmas holiday period (i.e. from 28 December) unless their owners paid them a wage for their work.

Sam Sharpe organized the protest through leading or co-ordinating a series of meetings for Bible study and prayer with the enslaved across a number of estates. He is recorded as indicating to those that intended to be a part of the 'sit-down' strike, that they had to first take an oath by kissing the Bible. He is also recorded as saying that on reading his Bible he could see that the white man had no more right to enslave black people than black people had to enslave the white man.

The protest is believed to have spanned an area of over 700 square miles and involved more than 60,000 enslaved persons. The 'sit-down' strike was also accompanied by the actions of some who chose to go against Sam Sharpe's non-violent plans of resistance, and set fire to estates and attacked estate owners. The protest is believed to have lasted about 10 days. In all it is estimated that more than 500 enslaved persons were killed or executed, and many more subject to savage beatings throughout the protest period. In contrast it is believed that 14 white estate owners died during the protest.

Sam Sharpe, for his part in the protest, was executed by the ruling British government on 23 May 1832, in Jamaica.

In 1975, Sam Sharpe was made one of the National Heroes of Jamaica and given the title of 'The Right Excellent' in recognition of the impact of the protest he led, which hastened the abolition of slavery. The 'Act for the Abolition of Slavery' was passed on 28 August 1833.

Further Reading

Larry J. Kreitzer, *"Kissing the Book": The Story of Sam Sharpe as Revealed in the Records of the National Archives at Kew*. Centre for Baptist History and Heritage Studies, Occasional Papers 7 (Oxford: Regent's Park College, 2013).

Horace O. Russell, *Samuel Sharpe and the Meaning of Freedom. Reflections on a Baptist National Hero of Jamaica*. Centre for Baptist History and Heritage Studies, Occasional Papers 5 (Oxford: Regent's Park College, 2012).

Delroy Reid-Salmon, *Burning for Freedom. A Theology of the Black Atlantic Struggle for Liberation* (Kingston: Ian Randle Publishers, 2012).

Jamaica Information Service: http://jis.gov.jm/heroes/samuel-sharpe/.

Study 5. Peter Stanford.
Reaching Out to the Margins

Opening Prayer

This can be based around a suitably justice-focused text such as: Psalm 146 or Micah 6:8.

Introduction

Take time to answer the following question:
- In what year to do you think Birmingham in England had its first black pastor?

Make a note of your answer.

The story of Peter Stanford

- Watch a short biography of Peter Thomas Stanford such as the one that appears on www.vimeo.com and take the time to read the short, written biography on Peter Stanford contained on the next few pages of this resource.
- Once you have done this, reflect on anything you have discovered about Peter Stanford that surprises you.

Peter Stanford's connection with sermons in the Gospel of Matthew

The Revd. Peter Stanford founded a home for orphaned girls. He explained that the aim of the institution was to provide for orphaned and neglected children of the rural districts of the Southern United States. This was to give them normal education and training for industrial work, and also to provide a temporary home for girls of colour who came to Boston and its vicinity.

He made his spiritual motivation for doing this clear by re-using words from the sermon recorded as delivered by Jesus, which is contained in Matthew 25:31-46: 'Feed the hungry' and 'Clothe the naked'. He added from the next chapter of Matthew (26:11), 'The poor you always have with you.'

Read Matthew 25:31-46 and as you reflect on it keep the following question in mind:

- Who is the text being addressed to?
- What behaviour is being deemed unacceptable?
- What behaviour is being deemed acceptable?
- Why might Peter Stanford have seen this text as being so significant?

Some things we know about the Gospel of Matthew

This Gospel is distinctive from the other Gospel accounts in that it contains five detailed sermons recorded as being delivered by Jesus, which cover several chapters of the book, as follows: Matthew 5:1–7:29; 10:1-42; 13:1-52; 18:1-35; 24:1–25:46. The last of those five sermons focuses very much on the 'end times' and being ready for when Jesus returns.

In particular the passage in Matthew 25:31-46 focuses on 'the final judgment' of people based on their treatment of those on the margins of society.

Why Peter Stanford might have seen Matthew 25:31-46 as being so important

As a pastor serving in many cities in the USA, Canada and Britain – including Hamilton, London, Birmingham, Bradford, Boston and New York – Peter Stanford witnessed a lot of need amongst people that was not being met. This text would clearly have been a reminder to him and others that looking after those in need was not simply a good thing to do but actually at the heart of being a Christian.

The relevance of Peter Stanford's story for 21st-century life

Identify a current issue that relates to the failure to care for those on the margins of society. For example, consider the people that die in police or prison custody under suspicious or suspected unlawful circumstances.

Then consider what an appropriate prophetic voice and action might look like on the issues, bearing in mind the example of the life of Peter Stanford. Do also consider what role you might personally play in bringing that prophetic voice and action to the issues.

Closing Worship

Listen to or sing the song 'Lift every voice and sing',[20] which is often referred to as the African-American national anthem. Then close with prayers of thanks for 19th-century and 20th-century prophets like Martin Luther King Jr, Mojola Agbebi, Nannie Helen Burroughs, Sam Sharpe and Peter Stanford, and for the legacy they have left us to build upon.

******

Biography of the Revd Peter Stanford
(by the Revd Dr Paul Walker)

The Revd Peter Thomas Stanford (1860–1909) was aged five at the end of the American Civil War which ended slavery, and as the plantation system broke down the orphaned boy was taken in by Native Americans, who taught him their language. They eventually passed him to a Quaker group who took him to an orphanage in Boston, from where he was adopted by a Mr and Mrs Stanford, coal merchants.

After what he describes in his life narrative, *From Bondage to Liberty*, as 5 years of ill-treatment, he ran away and eventually ended up living with a children's gang on the streets of New York City.

He was converted to Christian faith at a rally led by the well-known evangelists Moody and Sankey and came to the attention of some Christians who had been prominent in working for the abolition of slavery. They helped him to attend Suffield Baptist Institute, Connecticut, where he completed his studies before being ordained in 1878 as pastor of Zion Baptist Church, Hartford, Connecticut, a mission church for African Americans who had come from the Southern States before and after the emancipation of enslaved persons.

---

[20] For lyrics and music see: www.hymnary.org.

In 1882 Stanford went to Canada where he was briefly pastor of a church in Hamilton, Ontario and then of the Horton Street Baptist Church, London, Ontario, part of the Amherstburg African Baptist Association. During his time there he was editor of the *Christian Defender* newspaper.

He arrived in Liverpool in May 1883, hoping to raise funds for the struggling black church in Canada. After a few weeks Stanford went to London, where he was employed as an evangelist by a Revd Mr Baxter, editor of the *Christian Herald*, subsequently spending time in Bradford and Keighley, Yorkshire.

He settled in Birmingham in 1887. On August 13th 1888 he married an English woman, Beatrice Mabel Stickley, at the Baptist chapel in Smethwick. In May 1889, Stanford became the minister of Hope Street Baptist Chapel, Highgate, Birmingham.

Stanford took over another church in Priestly Rd, Sparkbrook, Birmingham, whilst continuing the work at Hope Street. It was his desire to 'express in some tangible form the gratification felt towards William Wilberforce, the great benefactor of the Negro' (his words), so they called it the Wilberforce Memorial Church.

Birmingham as a city had a world-wide reputation for justice, equality and enterprise, had been at the forefront of the campaign to abolish slavery and, after slavery ended in the States, had many organizations which supported the freed slaves.

In the 1890s Birmingham became a centre of the campaign against the lynchings of African Americans. Stanford was well known as 'Birmingham's Coloured Preacher' so would have been an obvious choice when anti-lynching campaigners in Birmingham wanted someone to go to the USA and report on the lynchings. Thus at a public meeting in May 1894 it was resolved that Stanford should visit the States and report on the situation facing the freed African-Americans.

In September 1895 Stanford returned to Boston, Massachusetts. His investigation into lynchings revealed that, despite emancipation, the injustices black people faced were terrible. He discovered that the number and form of lynchings were worse than the reports in England indicated. After his investigation Stanford published his book *The Tragedy of the Negro in America* in which he gave details of how African people arrived in America, the injustice they suffered in slavery, and the horror of lynchings.

At the same time as he was researching lynchings, Stanford founded St. Mark Congregational Church, Roxbury, Boston, the first African-American church in that district. He was an early ecumenist and organized the Interdenominational Ministers Association in Boston. From St Mark, Stanford went briefly to minister in New York City. He returned to North Cambridge, Massachusetts and founded the Union Industrial and Stranger's Home for homeless women and children. He served as Vice-President of Christ's Medical and Theological College, Baltimore and as the Vice President for Massachusetts in the National Baptist Convention.

He died on May 20 1909 of kidney failure.

Further Reading
Peter Thomas Stanford, *The Tragedy of the Negro in America* (1897). Available at http://docsouth.unc.edu/church/stanford/frontis.html
Peter Thomas Stanford, *Imaginary Obstructions to True Spiritual Progress* (1898). Available at The Library of Congress web site, http://memory.loc.gov.
Peter Thomas Stanford, *From Bondage to Liberty* (1889), in Birmingham City Archives.
Paul Walker, *The Revd Peter Thomas Stanford (1860-1909) Birmingham's Coloured Preacher*, PhD, Manchester University, 2004.

Made in the USA
Columbia, SC
01 November 2023